Popular Culture:

1940–1959

Nick Hunter

Chicago, Illinois

www.capstonepub.com
Visit our website to find out more information about Heinemann-Raintree books.

To order:
☎ Phone 800-747-4992
🖳 Visit www.capstonepub.com to browse our catalog and order online.

Edited by Adam Miller, Andrew Farrow, and Adrian Vigliano
Designed by Richard Parker
Original illustrations © Capstone Global
  Ltd 2012
Illustrations by Richard Parker
Picture research by Mica Brancic
Originated by Capstone Global Library Ltd
Printed and bound in China by Leo Paper
  Products Ltd

16 15 14 13 12
10 9 8 7 6 5 4 3 2 1

Library of Congress Cataloging-in-Publication Data
Hunter, Nick.
  Popular culture : 1940-1959 / Nick Hunter.
    p. cm.—(A history of popular culture)
  Includes bibliographical references and index.
  ISBN 978-1-4109-4623-2 (hb)—ISBN 978-1-4109-4630-0 (pb) 1. Popular culture—United States—History—20th century—Juvenile literature. 2. United States—Civilization—1945—Juvenile literature. 3. United States—Civilization—1918-1945—Juvenile literature. 4. United States—Social life and customs—1945-1970—Juvenile literature. 5. United States—Social life and customs—1918-1945—Juvenile literature. I. Title. II. Title: 1940-1959.
  E169.Z8H8457 2013
  973.91—dc23   2011038609

Acknowledgments
We would like to thank the following for permission to reproduce photographs: Getty Images pp. 5 (Hulton Archive), 6 (Time Life Pictures/William Vandivert), 7 (Archive Photos/Lambert), 9 (Hulton Archive/Retrofile/George Marks), 11 (Popperfoto), 13 (Time & Life Pictures/J R Eyerman), 14 (Moviepix/John Kobal Foundation), 17, 31, 52 (Michael Ochs Archives), 18, 27 (Hulton Archive), 19 (Hulton Archive/Harold Clements), 21 (Archive Photos/Harold M Lambert), 23 (CBS Photo Archive), 22 (Hulton Archive/Fox Photos/William Vanderson), 25 (Moviepix/Silver Screen Collection), 28 (Hulton Archive/Keystone Features/John Drysdale), 24 (Time & Life Pictures/Carl Mydans), 30 (Michael Ochs Archives/James Kriegsmann), 33 (Redferns/RB), 35 (Moviepix/Silver Screen Collection), 37 (Archive Photos/Tom Kelley), 39, 41, 50 (Hulton Archive/Apic), 44 (Hulton Archive/Thurston Hopkins), 47 (Moviepix/Michael Ochs Archives), 48 (Time Life Pictures/Carl Iwasaki [Popperfoto]), 49 (Hulton Archive/BIPs/Juliette Lasserre); Photoshot pp. 34 (© UPPA), 51 (© Starstock); Rex Features pp. 12 (GTV Archive), 43 (Everett Collection). Background images and design features reproduced with permission of Shutterstock.

Cover photograph of a young couple snuggling reproduced with the permission of Getty Images (Time & Life Pictures/J. R. Eyerman).

Every effort has been made to contact copyright holders of any material reproduced in this book. Any omissions will be rectified in subsequent printings if notice is given to the publisher.

Disclaimer
All the Internet addresses (URLs) given in this book were valid at the time of going to press. However, due to the dynamic nature of the Internet, some addresses may have changed, or sites may have changed or ceased to exist since publication. While the author and publisher regret any inconvenience this may cause readers, no responsibility for any such changes can be accepted by either the author or the publisher.

Contents

Some words are printed in bold, **like this**. You can find out what they mean by looking in the glossary.

What Is Popular Culture?

On the evening of September 9, 1956, eight out of ten people watching television in America were tuned into *The Ed Sullivan Show*. The awestruck studio audience and millions watching at home had not tuned in to see the show's host. Ed Sullivan was not even appearing that night. They all wanted to catch a glimpse of a young singer from Memphis, Tennessee. Elvis Presley was already hugely popular with young people and his appearance on the show was a major step in establishing him as one of the most famous faces, and voices, in the history of popular culture.[1]

Presley's music and the huge numbers of people he could reach through the new **medium** of TV are examples of pop culture at its most exciting. Pop, or popular, culture is designed to be seen or heard by as many people as possible. It appeals to the general public, or a section of the general public, rather than a cultural elite. Pop culture includes films, music, magazines, and even advertisements. Even the design styles of products such as cars and household appliances can be part of pop culture, because they are produced to appeal to people as desirable as well as useful objects.

Most of the things we think of as popular culture began to develop from the late nineteenth century. Just as industrial processes and new forms of transportation enabled **consumer** goods to be produced in huge numbers and distributed around a country or across the world, these changes also enabled culture such as films and music to be circulated in the same way. Before that time, culture was aimed at wealthy people in cities who attended theaters or concert halls, or was produced by people on a local scale to entertain friends and neighbors.

Mass media culture

Pop culture as we know it today would be impossible without electronic mass media like radio and TV to distribute it to a wider audience. Mass media means that huge numbers of people can be aware of cultural trends and products at the same time, such as when hearing a song on the radio or watching a popular program on TV.

Postwar pop culture

The 1940s and 1950s were an important period in the development of pop culture as we know it today. World War II raged from 1939 to 1945, claiming millions of lives and bringing huge changes to societies around the world. The outbreak of war had temporarily halted the development of a new medium of communication that would bring popular culture into people's home as never before. Televisions were very rare in the 1940s, but by 1959 they had become established as part of living rooms across the world. The period also saw changes in technology and society that influenced and, in turn, were influenced by popular culture.

When World War II came to an end, cinemas and dance halls were the main places to go for entertainment.

Did you know?

Today we take for granted that pop culture is often produced, distributed, and consumed using computers and the Internet. In the 40s and 50s, computers were huge machines used by governments and the military. One of the first electronic computers, unveiled in 1946, weighed 30 tons and had a tiny fraction of the processing power of even the simplest modern PC.[2]

Culture in the Shadow of War

The 1940s were dominated by World War II. Popular culture of the period was profoundly affected, whether in reflecting the horrors of the war itself or in giving people a way to forget about the war and the dangers that they and their loved ones faced. In order to win the war, countries had to put all their resources behind the effort. Some forms of culture, like Britain's early TV station, were shut down for the duration of the war.[1] Others, including radio and many films, were used to boost **morale** or deliver **propaganda** about the war effort.

The Holocaust

The war cast a long shadow over popular culture. Nazi Germany's **persecution** of Jews had led many to seek refuge overseas before the war, especially in the United States. These Jewish immigrants were often highly educated and creative, and they had a strong influence on postwar culture. The **Holocaust**, in which the Nazis murdered more than six million Jews, homosexuals, gypsies, and others, also had a big effect on culture in general as artists struggled to come to terms with and explain the Nazis' horrific crimes.

World War II affected the whole population more than any previous war had, as cities across Europe, including London (shown here), were bombed by enemy aircraft.

Social changes in wartime

The war had a major social impact. While men were away fighting in the war, more women joined the workforce. Many women became more confident of their own independence, and this was reflected in films and other cultural forms. International travel was rare at the time, so the arrival of more than a million U.S. troops in the United Kingdom and Europe to fight the war meant that Europeans learned more about American popular culture than ever before.

The 1940s was a time of shortages and **austerity** in many countries, because trade and industry had been disrupted by the war. Many goods were **rationed** in the U.S. during the war, and in Britain until 1954.[2] This was reflected in films and other popular culture of the time.

Men returned from fighting in the war to find major changes in many women's roles in society.

Dame Vera Lynn (b. Vera Welch, 1917-)

London-born singer Vera Lynn was known as the Forces' Sweetheart because of the role her songs played in raising British morale during the darkest days of World War II. After joining a musical troupe at the age of 11, Lynn went on to sing with several big bands in the 1930s. During the war, she recorded the radio series *Sincerely Yours* and played concerts for troops including popular songs such as "We'll Meet Again" and "The White Cliffs of Dover." After the war, Lynn had success in the United States, where she was the first UK female singer to have a number one hit, with "Auf Wiederseh'n Sweetheart" in 1952. Vera Lynn was honored as a Dame of the British Empire in 1975.[3]

The Cold War

World War II ended with the U.S. military dropping two atomic bombs on the Japanese cities of Hiroshima and Nagasaki, killing thousands of people in an instant. Within a few years, the Soviet Union also built an atomic bomb. Nuclear weapons meant that any conflict between the United States and the Soviet Union would be more destructive than any previous conflict. These two superpowers and their allies faced each other in a hostile standoff that became known as the **Cold War**.

Both sides in the Cold War were strongly opposed to the system of government of their opponents. Western governments and media opposed the **communist** belief that all areas of life should be controlled by the state, while the Soviet Union criticized the **consumerism** of the West. Both sides feared that the other was trying to undermine their way of life. This mistrust was shown in many smaller conflicts such as the Korean War (1950–1953).

Technology and society

In the years after World War II, the United States became unquestionably the world's largest economy, as European nations focused on reconstructing their shattered countries. America's factories that had produced arms and technology for the war effort switched to producing consumer goods. Science and technology had been pushed to the limit as nations strained to gain an advantage in World War II. This continued in the Cold War but technology also brought benefits. Fast travel by plane between and across continents was starting to become a reality for many people, although it was still very expensive. Kitchen appliances such as refrigerators became widespread, and cars were seen as essential rather than just a luxury.

Pop culture under communism

In the years that followed World War II, many countries in Eastern Europe, such as Hungary and Poland, were ruled by communist regimes that were dominated by and closely allied with the Soviet Union. These regimes were determined to control all aspects of their people's lives. Anyone who criticized the government was arrested. Films and other types of popular culture were heavily biased toward the government and support of the communist system, and Western culture and society were routinely criticized.

Although many more women had worked outside the home during the war, the 1950s saw some return to the traditional family roles that had existed before the war, with women looking after home and family while men went out to work.

The battle for civil rights

African Americans were also looking for change in the 1950s, particularly in the southern states of the United States. In 1955, Rosa Parks of Montgomery, Alabama, was fined $10 for boarding a bus and refusing to give up her seat for white passengers when the bus filled up. The African American people of Montgomery refused to use the city's buses until **segregation** was ended. In 1956, they won a victory when their leader, Martin Luther King Jr., was able to sit wherever he chose.[4] This was a small victory in the struggle for **civil rights** and **equality**, which would last into the 1960s and beyond.

Changes in technology led to social change as car ownership enabled people to move out of cities into spacious suburbs.

Going to the Movies

When World War II came to an end, going to the movies was at the heart of popular culture. Many people went to the movie theater once or even twice a week, not just to see the latest films from Hollywood but also to catch up on the news. The vast majority of people had no access to TV, so newsreel films pulled together news and sports that would be shown at the movies before the film started.

The film industry at war

The war made it very difficult to produce films in many countries. In the UK, much of the studio space was used to make propaganda and public information films for the government.[1] The French film industry came under the control of the occupying Germans and **censorship** severely restricted the types of films that could be made. In Germany itself film production continued, but filmmakers were not free to express their own views. Many films contained propaganda or promoted the Nazis' **racist** views, such as their bias against Jews.

In Hollywood, far away from the main war zones in Europe and Asia, the war years provided a boost to the film industry. Film production had declined in the 1930s because of the **Great Depression**, but jobs in war industries meant that many people now had more money in their pockets. People turned to the cinema for news from around the world but also to take their minds off the horrors of the conflict. Hollywood also benefitted from the arrival of creative talents fleeing the war in Europe, such as Austrian-born writer and **director** Billy Wilder, who had a hugely successful career in Hollywood after leaving his home to escape Nazi persecution.

Although many of the films made during the 1940s had wartime themes, the most popular films were often about **escapism**. Walt Disney's cartoon films such as *Fantasia* (1940) and *Bambi* (1942) attracted huge audiences and sold-out theaters. Films also reflected changes in wider society. As men went to fight in the war, women were doing jobs that had been filled by men before the war, as well as looking after a home and family. Films reflected these changes with strong female **role models** in films like *Now, Voyager* (1942), in which Bette Davis plays a young woman who escapes her background to become confident and independent, and finds love along the way.

Films as propaganda

Popular films were often used to raise morale and criticize the opposition during the war. Hollywood films like Charlie Chaplin's *The Great Dictator* (1940) and *Casablanca* (1942), set in wartime Morocco, gave a favorable view of democracies like Britain and the United States and were viewed as attacks on Hitler's Germany and its allies. Laurence Olivier's film *Henry V* (1944), which was based on Shakespeare's play of the same name, recalled a heroic battle from Britain's past. Many British films were made with government support, such as *The First of the Few* (1942), which told the story of the Spitfire aircraft that was so important in winning the Battle of Britain in 1940.

Shakespeare's play *Henry V* tells the story of English troops triumphing on French soil, led by the inspirational King Henry. The film's director and star was Laurence Olivier, one of the greatest stage actors of all time. His film helped to raise morale for the Allied invasion of Nazi-occupied Europe in 1944.

Did you know?

There were more moviegoers in 1946 than in any year before or since, with more than 1.6 billion tickets sold in the war-ravaged United Kingdom alone.[2]

Postwar Hollywood

The end of the war meant that there were more opportunities to sell Hollywood films internationally. Both Britain and France imposed taxes and other restrictions on foreign films to protect their local film industries. Propaganda also continued after the war. Defeated countries like Japan and the parts of Germany not controlled by the Soviet Union showed American films as examples of how a **democratic** and **capitalist** society should operate.

After the record numbers of 1946, attendance at the movies declined during the later 1940s and then dropped dramatically in the 1950s as more families had TVs at home. The way Hollywood operated also changed. In the 1930s, many theaters had been owned by Hollywood studios. However, this became illegal, meaning that studios now had to compete with each other to get their films shown in theaters. This meant that fewer films were made and more money was spent on each one to try to make it a success. This marked the start of the big-budget **blockbuster** film.

Making movies special

As TVs became widespread in the 1950s, the film industry had to come up with new ideas to tempt people away from their small screens. Movie theaters still had plenty of advantages, because TV pictures were often fuzzy and only available in black and white, compared with the clear, color images on the big screen. CinemaScope was introduced in 1953, using a special lens to make the big screen image even bigger. Another innovation was the 3-D film, which directors used to show images of animals and vehicles coming out of the screen toward the viewer.

At the box office, Walt Disney's cartoons were the most popular films of both the 1940s and the 1950s, with *Lady and the Tramp* (1955), *Peter Pan* (1953), and *Cinderella* (1950) the biggest hits of the next decade. This still is from the hit film *Bambi* (1942).

HUAC and the Hollywood Ten

As Cold War tensions rose between the United States and the Soviet Union, the House Un-American Activities Committee (HUAC) claimed that there were communists in Hollywood intent on producing pro-communist films. Ten filmmakers and actors refused to answer the committee's questions about whether they had communist sympathies, and they were jailed as a result. They were among many people in the 1940s and 1950s who had their careers wrecked because of anti-communist "**witch hunts**." Many of Hollywood's biggest stars protested against the actions of HUAC, but others, including actor and future U.S. president Ronald Reagan, supported the committee and even informed on their colleagues.[3] In the 1950s, the fight against supposed communists was taken up by the notorious Senator Joseph McCarthy.

Viewers had to wear cardboard glasses with special lenses to watch 3-D films. This was not a comfortable way to watch movies, and the craze passed after a few years.

Most Popular Films of the 1940s[4]

1. *Bambi* (1942)—Walt Disney animated feature film
2. *Pinocchio* (1940)—Walt Disney animated feature film
3. *Fantasia* (1940)—Walt Disney animated feature film
4. *Song of the South* (1946)—Walt Disney live-action and animated feature film
5. *Mom and Dad* (1945)—Drama
6. *Samson and Delilah* (1949)—Biblical drama starring Hedy Lamarr and Victor Mature
7. *The Best Years of Our Lives* (1946)—Drama starring Fredric March and Myrna Loy
8. *The Bells of St. Mary's* (1945)—Drama starring Bing Crosby and Ingrid Bergman
9. *Duel in the Sun* (1946)—Western starring Jennifer Jones, Joseph Cotton, and Gregory Peck
10. *This Is the Army* (1943)—Musical comedy

What did people watch?

In 1941, a film was released that many experts still think is the best film ever made. Directed by the young Orson Welles, *Citizen Kane* told the story of a newspaper **tycoon**. Critics have heaped praise on the film ever since, but it would not appear on any list of the most-watched films of the period. That list was dominated by the feature-length cartoons of Walt Disney, which captivated audiences at the time and remain popular today.

There were many other genres, or types, of films that became popular during the period. Film noir (meaning "black film") was at its height in the 1940s with movies such as *Double Indemnity* (1944) and *The Big Sleep* (1946). The genre's name came from the low lighting and shadows that gave these films a mysterious and brooding atmosphere. They were often based on popular crime fiction such as the works of Raymond Chandler, and dealt with crime and double-dealing in the mean streets of U.S. cities. They reflected the worries of the time about wars such as the Cold War. The lead character was often an outsider or loner, which was also a feature of another popular genre that flourished in the 1950s—the western.

At the opposite end of the spectrum was the growth of the film musical. Bigger budgets for blockbuster movies meant that the lavish costumes and sets of the musicals that people could see on **Broadway** could now be brought to the big screen. Some musicals, like Gene Kelly's *Singin' in the Rain* (1952), were specifically written for the movies. Many others, including *Oklahoma!* (1955) and *South Pacific* (1958), were adapted versions of Broadway hits, which had already proved their appeal to audiences. Comedy was also popular, from the visual comedy of Abbott and Costello to the more sophisticated comedies about love and relationships such as *Adam's Rib* (1949), starring Katharine Hepburn and Spencer Tracy.

Did you know?

Not every film made in the 1950s was a success. Edward Wood was renowned as one of the worst directors of all time, and his film *Plan 9 From Outer Space* (1959) was so bad that it became a "so bad it's good" **cult** hit. Wood's other projects, including horror films starring Bela Lugosi, were not much better. Wood was so notorious that his life was later made into a film starring Johnny Depp.

Humphrey Bogart and Lauren Bacall were one of Hollywood's most successful partnerships, both on and off screen. They were married in 1945, after meeting on the set of *To Have and Have Not* (1944).[6]

Alfred Hitchcock (1899-1980)

Alfred Hitchcock was born in London and began his career in the United Kingdom. He started working on silent films in 1920. Hitchcock made his reputation directing films such as *The Lady Vanishes* (1938). He moved to Hollywood to direct *Rebecca* (1940), which won an **Oscar** for Best Picture. Hitchcock spent the rest of his career in the United States, and is best known for making suspense thrillers including *Rear Window* (1954), *Vertigo* (1958), and *Psycho* (1960). He was famous for appearing in small roles in each of his films. Hitchcock's fame was cemented by the series *Alfred Hitchcock Presents*, which he produced for TV starting in the late 1950s.[5]

Shooting stars

Hollywood's top actors and actresses were the biggest stars in the world, from sophisticated stars like Cary Grant and Rita Hayworth to the charming tough guys like John Wayne, who dominated the western genre in this period. One of Hollywood's leading ladies, Grace Kelly, even became royalty when she married Prince Rainier of Monaco in 1956.[7]

During World War II, some Hollywood stars, such as James Stewart, joined the armed forces. Others spent the war entertaining troops. After the war, the role of the star was changing in Hollywood. Previously, most actors and directors had been under contract with the big studios, meaning that they had very little freedom regarding the films they could make. As studios searched for **box office** successes, they turned to more independent companies to make those films, giving the stars more freedom.

The next generation

In the 1950s, a new breed of stars emerged. Actors such as James Dean, Marlon Brando, and Marilyn Monroe were vulnerable and confused like real people, rather than impossibly glamorous like the stars of previous eras. Their films marked a new gritty realism in Hollywood. Films distinguished themselves from TV by tackling the more controversial subject matter that TV companies did not cover, such as the teenage rebellion of James Dean in *Rebel Without a Cause* (1955).

Movies around the world

Although Hollywood was the center of the film industry, there were notable films and film stars in many countries around the world. British films, including the popular Ealing comedies, reflected the realities of Britain during and after the war, but often found it difficult to compete with Hollywood. British directors and actors often achieved international success, including Alec Guinness, who graduated from Ealing comedies to star in *The Bridge on the River Kwai* (1957) and later appeared as Obi-Wan Kenobi in *Star Wars* (1977).

Other European countries, including Italy and France, were able to develop distinctive styles of film. Directors such as Italy's Federico Fellini and Japan's Akira Kurosawa were not just successful in their own countries, but had an influence around the world, including in Hollywood.

Drive-in movies

In the United States, a new viewing experience became hugely popular, and movie-goers did not even have to leave their cars. By 1956, drive-in theaters accounted for a quarter of ticket sales in the U.S. Many of the tickets were sold to teenagers, who could escape their parents' supervision for a few hours. Studios developed films specially for the drive-ins, focusing on cheap horror movies and subject matter that appealed to teenagers.[8]

Marilyn Monroe (1926-1962)

Born Norma Jean Mortenson in Los Angeles, California, Marilyn Monroe spent an unhappy childhood in orphanages and foster homes. Monroe's most famous films include *Gentlemen Prefer Blondes* (1953), *The Seven Year Itch* (1955), and *Some Like It Hot* (1959), in which she combined beauty and a sense of humor to become a screen icon. She struggled with relentless media attention as she tried to take on less typical roles in later films. Monroe died after taking an overdose of sleeping pills in 1962, which only increased her legend as the tragic star of a golden era.

Home Entertainment

If one area of popular culture changed beyond recognition in the 1940s and 1950s, it was home entertainment. In 1940, a committee was formed in the United States to agree on standards for TV transmissions.[1] By 1960, TVs were so common that John F. Kennedy's relaxed appearance on TV opposite Richard Nixon was seen as one of the main reasons why he won the election to be president. As discussed in the previous chapter, TV was strong competition for the movies, but it also affected every other area of popular culture, from music to advertising, during the period.

Radio days

Before TV became widespread in the 1950s, most people got their news and entertainment from the radio. Radios were not portable like they are today, so a family might sit around the radio to listen to favorite programs. In the United States these included **variety shows** hosted by popular comedians such as Red Skelton and Bob Hope. In the United Kingdom the show *Dick Barton—Special Agent* attracted 15 million listeners every evening.[2]

American radio developed into four different **networks**, including CBS, NBC, and ABC, all of which would later move into the new medium of TV. These networks created programming for local stations across the country that would broadcast music but also drama, comedy, and sports. As TV became dominant in the late 1950s, these companies stopped producing network radio programs. Radio programming became mainly a mix of music and advertising.

Bob Hope was a star of radio, movies, and television. He was also famous for entertaining troops in conflicts from World War II to the Korean and Vietnam Wars.

Not all countries adopted the U.S. **commercial** model. British radio was dominated by the British Broadcasting Corporation (BBC), which was the only official broadcaster. The BBC was, and still is, funded by a license fee, which meant it was independent of direct state funding and political influence. Other countries followed similar models or, as in Canada, had a mix of commercial and national broadcasters.[3]

Did you know?

The BBC broadcast a wide range of programs but avoided controversy. In 1947, the corporation declared that there would be only "an impartial account" of any issues being debated in parliament at the time or that might be debated in the near future.[4]

The Goon Show was a BBC radio comedy that was distributed around the world. Later performers who named it as an influence on their work included the Monty Python comedy team and John Lennon, who said they were "proof that the world was insane."[6]

The transistor

Radio underwent its own technological revolution in the 1950s, following the invention of the **transistor** in 1947.[5] Until that time, radios had worked using vacuum tubes, which made them large and fragile. The radio typically sat in the corner of the family living room, much as the TV would in the decades that followed. Transistors made radios smaller and less easy to break, which in turn made them much more portable and more **versatile** than TVs for use in cars and on the move. Transistors also revolutionized other areas of electronics and played a vital part in the development of computers.

Moving pictures at home

The first TV service started in the United Kingdom in 1936. Even though 20,000 new TVs had been sold in London, the service was closed when war broke out in September 1939, making these TVs useless until broadcasting resumed after the war. Although commercial TV was first broadcast in the United States in 1941, it wasn't very widespread until 1945.

At first it did not seem that TV would catch on. Only 8,000 sets had been sold in the United States by the end of 1946, as networks argued about the shape the new medium would take.[7] Questions were raised about whether TV took up too much of people's attention so they would not have time to do other things, such as they could do when listening to the radio. Television was very expensive to produce, and people asked whether advertisers would be prepared to pay for it. The doubts did not last long, and in 1948, *Newsweek* magazine reported that television was "catching on like a case of high-toned scarlet fever."[8]

Technical issues and the money required to make programs meant that the radio networks such as NBC and CBS were able to establish a dominance that lasted for many decades. In the United Kingdom, the BBC was the only television service in the 1940s. The medium really took off in 1953, when many people bought their first televisions to watch the coronation of Queen Elizabeth II.[9] The Independent Television Authority was formed in 1954 to develop commercial competition for the BBC.[10]

TV technology

One of the biggest problems in the early days of television was establishing a standard system for broadcasting TV pictures that everyone could use. The United States and Europe established slightly different standards, and most other countries followed one or the other.[11] The first pictures were in black and white, and the next step was to develop a color system. The first color TVs were produced in 1954 in the United States, although they were not widespread until the 1960s.

Early TV programs were usually broadcast live, because recording them on film was a costly and complex process. In the mid-1950s, a system was developed to record programs onto magnetic tape, which was much simpler and less expensive than using film. This revolutionized television, because local stations could now show programs at different times. Also, these programs could be sold to other TV companies around the world.

Cowboy series were popular features on TV in the 1950s.

Did you know?

In 1947, there were fewer TVs in the United States than there were movie theaters. By the mid-1950s more than 32 million Americans had purchased TVs.

Quote

"Why should people go out and pay money to see bad films when they can stay at home and see bad television for nothing."
Samuel Goldwyn, Hollywood studio owner[12]

Stars and scheduling

Many of the programs on the new TV channels transferred directly from radio, including variety and comedy shows. Popular TV variety shows included Milton Berle's *Texaco Star Theater* and *The Ed Sullivan Show*.

In the early days of television, plays were performed live on TV featuring theater actors. However, as recording technology developed, the kinds of drama on TV also changed. Production moved to Hollywood as film companies realized there was money to be made from television, and one-off dramas were replaced by series. Series were easier to schedule and cheaper to produce, because one film set or group of actors could fill many hours of television. Advertisers could target series that appealed to the people they wanted to buy their products. Popular series included the police drama *Dragnet* and the western series *Gunsmoke*.

Like Hollywood serials, situation comedies could also be produced in long series with recognizable characters. In the 1950s, sitcoms were often based around well-known personalities such as Lucille Ball or, in the United Kingdom, Tony Hancock, who starred in *Hancock's Half Hour*. Their characters were exaggerated versions of themselves. Quiz shows were another inexpensive way of creating tension and entertainment. Quiz show formats such as *The $64,000 Question* were sold around the world. There was outrage when it was disclosed that quiz shows were not always as spontaneous as they seemed. Sometimes contestants were fed answers in advance so that the TV companies would control the results. Eventually changes were made to stop this from happening.

Live news broadcasts and discussions replaced the newsreels that had existed before television.

Family entertainment

Viewers had a limited choice of channels and programs in the 1950s. It was important to TV companies and advertisers that they appealed to as many people as possible. Sitcoms such as *The Honeymooners*, starring Jackie Gleason, showed everyday family groups who landed themselves in comical situations but always resolved things by the end of the show. For culture that confronted difficult social issues, people had to look elsewhere.

Lucille Ball (1911-1989)

Lucille Ball's most famous character, Lucy (shown above left), was a dizzy housewife who longed to be in show business. In reality, Ball was a TV pioneer and one of the most successful women in the medium's history. Ball starred in many Hollywood films during the 1930s and 1940s, during which time she met and married Cuban bandleader Desi Arnaz.

In 1951, Ball was asked to develop a show for television. *I Love Lucy*, starring Ball and Arnaz, was an instant success, and new recording technology meant the show could be aired repeatedly and sold around the world. At the show's peak between 1952 and 1953, it was watched by more than two-thirds of the television audience.[13] It was one of the first shows designed specifically for television, using three cameras so the scene could be shot from different angles. The show was renamed *The Lucille Ball-Desi Arnaz Show* in 1957. After the final season in 1958, Ball's production company continued to produce shows for her and others to star in.[14]

Music

During World War II, the most popular form of music was big band swing, as performed by artists including Glenn Miller and Benny Goodman. The decades that followed saw the growth of many different musical styles, from the golden age of Broadway musicals, to country and blues from the southern United States, to rock-and-roll music that conquered the world in the late 1950s. This change can be credited partly to some of the greatest musicians and performers ever seen, but also owed much to changes in technology and society.

The swinging 1940s

Before World War II, record sales had overtaken sheet music as the main way that music was consumed. Big bands became some of the first big stars of recorded music. This music featured mainly brass and woodwind instruments and took its inspiration from jazz. It differed from jazz, however, by giving musicians less freedom to express themselves through improvisation.

The most original big band music was played by African American musicians such as Duke Ellington, but racial prejudice meant that white acts were booked in the best dance halls and received more radio exposure.[1] As a result, white bands achieved wider popularity with the majority white populations in North America and Europe.

During and after World War II, dance halls were packed with couples dancing to big band music.

Big bands continued to be popular throughout the 1940s but were overtaken in popularity by solo singers. Bing Crosby had been the most successful prewar singer, and he provided inspiration for new stars including Perry Como and big band graduate Frank Sinatra.

Frank Sinatra (1915-1998)

Frank Sinatra was probably the greatest singer of the immediate postwar period. His career began as a singer for big bands, including Tommy Dorsey's and Harry James's. As his popularity grew, he left Dorsey's band in 1942. This was a big risk, because very few singers could make it on their own at this time, but Sinatra attracted a huge following, particularly among teenage girls. After great success with Columbia Records in the 1940s, his career declined in the early 1950s.

Sinatra also made a name for himself as an actor in films including *From Here to Eternity* (1954), for which he won an Oscar. Acting roles like this revived his career, and he recorded some of his greatest music for Capitol Records between 1953 and 1962. Some of those albums include *Songs for Swingin' Lovers* (1956) and *Come Fly With Me* (1958). As one of the first superstar singers, Sinatra's private life attracted huge media attention and there were persistent rumors of friendships with leaders of organized crime gangs.[2]

Quote

"It was the war years, and there was a great loneliness. And I was the boy in every corner drug-store ... who'd gone off, drafted to the war. That was all."

Frank Sinatra explains the reasons for his popularity in the 1940s[3]

Dance halls and dancing

The success of big band swing also led to new dance styles. Big bands played in hotels and dance halls, and a night out dancing the boogie-woogie or the jitterbug became as popular as going to the movies. What made these different from earlier dances was that partners did not hold each other in an embrace, like in ballroom dancing. Dancing became much less formal, allowing freer expression.

Latin styles of dancing such as the rumba and the samba had been popular before the war and these continued into the 1950s. Latin music was also influenced by jazz and swing, and the mambo developed as a dance for this changing music,[4] featuring bandleaders such as Tito Rodriguez and Tito Puente.

Musical theater

For many people the 1940s and 1950s were the golden age of the Broadway musical, with shows by Richard Rodgers and Oscar Hammerstein and others entrancing audiences around the world. These musicals remain popular many decades later. Musicals changed after the war, in that the songs were much more a part of the story and helped the development of the characters. Dance also became an important part of many musicals, such as Leonard Bernstein's *On the Town* (1944, filmed in 1949) and *West Side Story* (1957, filmed in 1961).[5]

One reason these musicals became so popular was because of changes outside the theaters. The long-playing record enabled recordings to be made, so people could listen to the show whether they were in New York or New Zealand. Recordings of musicals such as *South Pacific* on film and on record reached millions of people, whereas in an earlier era only theater-goers would have known the songs.

The success of Broadway overshadowed another major center for musicals—the West End of London. In 1943, at the same time Rodgers and Hammerstein's *Oklahoma!* was opening in New York, London had been badly damaged by wartime bombings, and theaters were playing musicals on wartime subjects to entertain troops and Londoners. Distinctly British musicals were produced by Ivor Novello and Noël Coward in the 1940s, who had both been popular before the war.[6] But there was huge excitement in 1947, when *Oklahoma!* became the first new American musical to open in the West End since before the war.

Rodgers and Hammerstein's greatest musicals received many awards and were successful on film and record, as well as on stages around the world.

Richard Rodgers (1902-1979) and Oscar Hammerstein II (1895-1960)

Rodgers and Hammerstein wrote some of the most famous musicals ever performed on Broadway. Rodgers wrote his first songs at the age of 11 and met his first great songwriting partner, Lorenz Hart, in 1918. Hart wrote lyrics to Rodgers's music for many musicals, including great songs such as "My Funny Valentine," before his early death in 1943. Rodgers teamed up with Hammerstein and changed musicals forever by making the songs part of the plot. Successes included *Oklahoma!* (1943); *Carousel* (1945); *South Pacific* (1949); *The King and I* (1951); and *The Sound of Music* (1959), which were also made into successful films.[7]

Country and folk

The growth of the recording industry and music radio in the United States helped the development of other types of music. Country, or hillbilly music as it was known in the early days, had originated in the rural southern United States. Its influence spread nationwide as people moved during the Great Depression of the 1930s and World War II. The cowboy style of Hollywood westerns also had an influence on country musicians. In 1949, *Billboard* magazine began to call this music country-and-western.[8] Hank Williams became country music's biggest star with his honky-tonk style using electric guitars and his distinctive yodeling singing style. It was also around 1950 that Nashville, Tennessee, became the center of the country music publishing and recording industry, as the genre became hugely popular in the United States and around the world.

Most folk music is not really part of popular culture. Whereas pop culture is developed to appeal and sell to a wide commercial audience, folk music develops within communities, such as the British and Irish folk songs that influenced country music, or the blues music that developed in southern African American communities after 1900. However, in the late 1950s, a middle-class, college-educated audience began to get interested in folk music. This ranged from the protest songs of Pete Seeger, who had been blacklisted for his communist sympathies, to the smoother, commercial sounds of the Kingston Trio. The Kingston Trio were clean-cut with short hair and designed to appeal to people who liked folk songs but found folk singers a little scruffy and political.

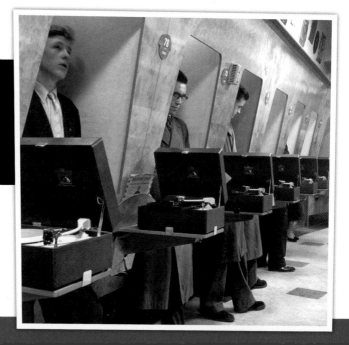

Customers in some record stores could listen to records in listening booths before deciding whether to buy them.

British skiffle boom

Although influenced by folk and jazz music, skiffle was mainly played by British musicians in the mid- to late 1950s. While most of the big stars of American music rarely visited the United Kingdom, skiffle's fast pace and strong rhythm was more relevant to young Britons, including future stars such as John Lennon and Paul McCartney, who played skiffle as teenagers before forming the Beatles. The most popular skiffle artist was Lonnie Donegan.

The revolutions revolution

One of the main reasons why recorded music became so popular was the development of vinyl records. Up until that point, recordings had been played on 78 revolutions per minute (rpm) discs. These were very fragile and could only play for a few minutes. In 1948, the 33 rpm long player was launched. It could play for around 30 minutes on each side, meaning several songs or longer pieces could fit on one disc. A smaller 45 rpm disc could play for a few minutes on each side and was an inexpensive way for people to buy a single song or recording.

Record sales in the U.S. increased dramatically during this period. This was partly because more people had access to records, but it also shows the popularity of new musical styles.

Did you know?

The word "skiffle" was first used in the United States to describe music played by people who were too poor to buy proper instruments and used improvised instruments like washboards and jugs instead.[9] This helped to make skiffle popular with young people who could not afford expensive instruments.

Rhythm and blues

Almost all pop and rock music produced since the mid-1950s can trace its roots back to the African American rhythm and blues (R&B) music that developed in the years after World War II. This music gave birth to rock, soul, and other forms of dance music that went on to dominate popular music for decades to come.

As the big bands of the war years declined or broke up, many of the most talented musicians, such as Dizzy Gillespie and Charlie Parker, started to develop a new type of jazz called bebop. This was beautiful, complex, uptempo music that featured lots of improvisation (solos that are made up on the spot), but it really wasn't designed for dancing. For fun and relaxation, African Americans turned to the "jump blues" of Louis Jordan. By the end of the 1940s, this music had developed so that it combined driving rhythms with the earthy lyrics of the blues music that had traveled from the rural south of the United States to cities like Memphis and Chicago. In 1949, *Billboard* magazine renamed their "race" music charts for music aimed at African American audiences as the rhythm and blues charts.[10]

Ray Charles (1930-2004)

Ray Charles's importance to the development of popular music is summed up by his nickname, the Genius. Born Ray Charles Robinson in Georgia, he lost his sight as a child but taught himself to play piano and to arrange and compose using Braille. Charles had a string of R&B hits in the early 1950s, including "Mess Around" (1953). He combined the rhythms and subject matter of rhythm and blues with the vocal style and passion of gospel music to create the first soul music with songs like "I Got a Woman" and "What'd I Say."[12] He later recorded jazz and country albums. Ray Charles also inspired other musicians with the control he had over his own career and the type of music he played at a time when this was unusual for African Americans.[13]

Louis Jordan (third from the left, holding a saxophone) is shown here with his group Tympany Five.

Rhythm and blues ranged from the electric blues of Muddy Waters to the music of Little Richard and Chuck Berry. It came to be viewed as part of the new rock and roll, by way of more jazz- or gospel-influenced artists like Ray Charles and Ruth Brown. Major record companies often ignored this new music, and independent record labels were created to sell it. These labels were often originated by groups of people, such as the Jewish Chess brothers of Chicago, who were also excluded by prejudice from other areas of business.

Crossing over

Rhythm and blues was aimed at African American audiences, but it had a much wider influence. Young people of all backgrounds sought out these exciting records instead of the diet of crooners and novelty records they were fed by mainstream radio. In 1953, a Los Angeles record store reported that 40 percent of the black music it sold was bought by white people.[11] The major labels tried to capitalize on R&B's popularity by recording pale imitations by Pat Boone and others, but rhythm and blues would soon find its way to the top of the mainstream charts.

Rock and roll

Alan Freed's *Moondog Rock 'n' Roll Party* radio show was a big hit with teenagers around Cleveland, Ohio, and played a big part in popularizing the phrase "rock 'n' roll." Freed used the term on his show to disguise the fact that he was playing the latest rhythm and blues songs to a mixed audience. When white musicians such as Elvis Presley began to combine rhythm and blues with elements of country music in a potent mix that became hugely popular with white teenagers, it was called rock and roll.

The early rock-and-roll hits of Presley and Bill Haley were often **cover versions** of rhythm and blues or country hits. Many of the other artists who played rock and roll wrote their own songs, including Chuck Berry, Little Richard, Buddy Holly, and Jerry Lee Lewis.

All shook up

At first the older generations were shocked by the pounding rhythms of rock and roll. The music was dismissed as a fad that would die out in a few years. To some extent this did happen as stars, including Elvis Presley, toned down their music to appeal to a wider audience. In 1959, Buddy Holly, another of the original rock and rollers, was killed in a plane crash that also claimed fellow musicians Ritchie Valens and the Big Bopper.

Rock around the world

The influence of rock and roll spread far beyond the southern United States. Those records spawned imitators such as Cliff Richard in the United Kingdom and Johnny Hallyday in France, but also fired up the imaginations of the next generation of musicians.

Did you know?

When Elvis Presley appeared on *The Ed Sullivan Show* in 1956, more than 80 percent of the U.S. TV audience was watching. He was shown from the waist up, because TV executives thought his hip-shaking dancing was indecent.[14]

Elvis Presley (1935-1977)

Elvis Presley came from a humble family in Tupelo, Mississippi. In 1954, he recorded a song for his mother and caught the attention of Memphis producer Sam Phillips.

Elvis's early recordings for Phillips's Sun Records caused a sensation in the local area. He signed to RCA records in 1955 and became one of the biggest recording stars of all time. He was called the King of Rock and Roll. Presley was not the first performer to combine country with rhythm and blues, but he was able to bring this music to a mass audience. By the time Presley was drafted into the army in 1958, he had played a major part in establishing rock and roll as a musical force. In the 1960s and 1970s, Presley moved away from pure rock and roll to become a movie star and family entertainer. He died of heart failure in 1977.

The electric guitar

Rock and roll could not have existed without the electric guitar. In the 1920s and 1930s, guitars that used electricity and amplifiers to make them louder had been used in jazz and country music. The first solid-bodied electric guitars were built around 1940, and the first solid-bodied electric guitar that was mass-produced was created by Leo Fender in 1948.

Design and Clothes

The war that raged around the world in 1940 had followed the longest and worst period of economic crisis in recent history—the Great Depression. Not surprisingly, when World War II finally came to an end, the world of style and design was ready to go through a period of major change. This was driven by technology, changes in society as a whole, and the fact that many people had more money to spend than they had in the past.

Although the war created jobs for many people who had been unemployed in the 1930s, including many more women, this did not mean that people could go out and buy new clothes. War production meant that factories were making war supplies rather than consumer goods. Like most things, clothing in Britain was in short supply, and rationing limited what people could buy even if they had money. A government campaign advised people to "Make Do and Mend."[1]

The new look

When the war came to an end, the fashion industry was able to rise from the ashes of a shattered Europe. Paris was eager to reestablish itself as the center of fashion. This was achieved by the bold "New Look" unveiled by Christian Dior. The flowing skirts and tight waists of the romantic New Look dresses brought a stylish end to the drabness of wartime. This was high fashion and beyond the reach of most people. However, this style became established as the look for the postwar period as Hollywood stars like Joan Crawford wore the styles on film and more affordable versions began to appear in department stores.

Christian Dior licensed versions of his designs that would be more affordable for more people.

Young style

Until the 1950s, young people had normally worn the same clothes as their parents. However, the good economic conditions of the 1950s meant that many young people now had jobs and money. They could afford to buy clothes and did not want to wear the same things as the older generation. Stores and clothing manufacturers began to cater specifically to these new consumers, who started to wear a distinctive style of clothes.

The outfit of the blue jeans and leather jacket worn by Marlon Brando in *The Wild One* was copied by many young people.

Christian Dior (1905-1957)

Christian Dior was the French designer who revived fashion after World War II. He restored the position of Paris as the capital of high fashion. Born in Normandy, France, Dior opened his salon in Paris in 1946 and unveiled the revolutionary New Look in 1947. In the decade that followed, he developed many more successful designs. When he died, Dior's assistant Yves Saint Laurent took over his fashion house.

New fabrics

During and after World War II, clothes began to be made of synthetic (chemically created) fibers such as nylon. The first nylon stockings were produced in 1939, and more than 64 million pairs were sold in the first year.[2] Synthetic fabrics meant that clothing could be produced more cheaply and could also be made more durable, for example, by making sure that dyes did not fade.

35

Consumer culture

It was not just in fashion that new design and materials were being used. In the 1950s, greater wealth and car ownership encouraged more people to move away from cities into the **suburbs**. Advertisers were eager to help people furnish their houses with the latest gadgets, such as refrigerators and washing machines. The design of these new devices was almost as important as their function.

The new consumer goods used bright colors, new plastic materials, and design features borrowed from car and aircraft design to convince buyers that their kitchen would be state of the art. Many of the elaborate curved designs for refrigerator doors and other appliances became design classics and very much part of the culture of the time.

More than just a car

The ultimate expression of 1950s design was in the automobile, and particularly the American automobile. Cars began to appear with elaborate tail fins, chrome bumpers, and other features that echoed aircraft design. Designs changed regularly to try to persuade consumers to buy the latest models. People bought these cars to express their affluence and confidence. Big American cars were much admired in other countries as they appeared on screen in Hollywood films, but car designers elsewhere tended to focus on practicality and economy more than the sheer style of American designers.

Pop art

Nineteen-fifties design and consumerism provided inspiration for a new art movement. Pop artists used images from popular culture, advertising, and comics to comment on the consumer culture they saw around them. Pioneers of early pop art included British artist Richard Hamilton, who created collages using images from advertising, as well as American artists Andy Warhol, Robert Rauschenberg, and Jasper Johns. The pop art movement had its greatest success in the 1960s.

Did you know?

In contrast to the huge American cars of the period, British designer Alec Issigonis created two of Britain's most popular small cars—the Morris Minor in 1948 and the Mini in 1959. The Mini was designed to be economic to run, and a huge number were sold in Britain before production ended. A modern version of the Mini was launched by BMW in 2001.[3]

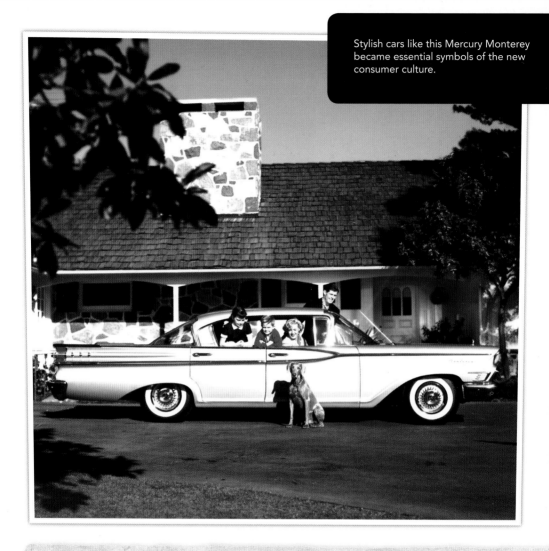

Stylish cars like this Mercury Monterey became essential symbols of the new consumer culture.

Japanese technology

New forms of popular culture, from television to records, needed equipment so that people could watch them and listen to them. Japan had been devastated in World War II, but set about rebuilding its economy and excelled in the manufacture of electronics, from the new transistor radios to TVs. Many companies focused on producing the best product at the lowest price, but at least one company, Sony, recognized the importance of how their products looked in appealing to design-conscious consumers.[4]

Advertising

The 1940s and 1950s gave advertisers more outlets for advertising than ever before, from the new medium of TV to billboards by the sides of increasingly busy roads. Newspapers and color magazines were also important for advertisers. The development of new consumer products gave advertisers more to advertise, and people's growing wealth in the 1950s meant they would buy more. Advertising reflects popular culture by using art and popular images to persuade people to buy things.

Before World War II, much of the advertising had been aimed at women, encouraging them to buy cleaning products and foods. In the **affluent** postwar period, advertising began to be aimed more at men, encouraging them to buy shaving products and, of course, cars. The images of men used in advertising were taken straight from Hollywood, and Hollywood stars were often used in advertising. Advertisements in all media still featured many traditional images of family life, with women pictured in the home and men shown going out to work.

Commercial break

The United States led the way in developing advertising for television. In the beginning, advertisers would sponsor a whole program or series. However, as the number of programs and channels grew, this became too expensive, and advertisers were concerned that they might end up sponsoring a whole series that was not a ratings success. TV networks were also worried that advertisers had too much control over programs. It worked best for everyone when advertising began to be sold in one-minute slots spread over several programs, as it still is today.

The effects of World War II made the United States the biggest economy in the world. American corporations used this strength to sell products on a global scale. The colors and logos of products like Coca-Cola were recognized around the world, and these products became global **brands**.

Did you know?

Television soap operas are long-running serials. The name comes from the fact that they were developed, for radio and later television, as a way for the advertisers that sponsored them to sell soap powder to female viewers and listeners. Early soap operas on U.S. television included *As the World Turns*, which was first broadcast in 1956.[5]

Advertising often promoted traditional ideas about the roles of men and women.

Wartime posters and propaganda

The techniques of advertising were used during wartime to recruit people into the armed forces, raise morale, and distribute government information. One U.S. poster during the war contained the slogan "Loose lips sink ships," which meant to be careful about revealing information that might give away secrets to the enemy and ultimately harm your own forces. Wartime posters produced by the British Ministry of Information were designed to be clear, to get their message across quickly, and to be easy to remember. Examples included "Keep it under your hat," advising people to beware of revealing information to possible enemy spies, and "Dig for victory" to persuade people to grow their own food.

The Printed Word

A new type of book had been introduced in the 1930s—the paperback. In the United States, paperbacks were usually printed on low-quality paper and were sold in drugstores and other outlets the way magazines were sold. In the United Kingdom, these were editions of popular classics published by Allen Lane's Penguin. Literature was more accessible than ever before.

Wartime best sellers

During World War II, paper rationing meant that very few new and popular titles were published in the United Kingdom. However, more books were being read than ever before.[1] Romance paperbacks were popular; particularly as many men were away from home fighting in the war so more books were sold to women. Wartime alliances affected what people read. American books, such as John Steinbeck's *The Grapes of Wrath*, became popular in the United Kingdom, and British authors, including A. J. Cronin, who wrote medical dramas, enjoyed unexpected popularity in the United States.

Titles about World War II appeared a few years after the war, including James Jones's *From Here to Eternity* and Alistair MacLean's *HMS Ulysses*. Most of these wartime best sellers were filmed, as were many other best-selling books of the period. The creation of blockbuster books affected the way films were being made. Religious stories like Lloyd C. Douglas's *The Robe* also got the Hollywood treatment, which boosted sales of the book on both sides of the Atlantic.

Postwar fiction

Crime fiction had been popular before the war, with many crime fiction novels filmed. A postwar success was Mickey Spillane's series about Mike Hammer, although the violence of these books and others like them was widely criticized.

The beat generation

Jazz was the major musical inspiration for the beat generation, which included writers such as Jack Kerouac, Allen Ginsberg, and William S. Burroughs. Their writings were designed to challenge the mainstream, using street language, their own experiences, and other ingredients such as Eastern religion. Their writings would go on to influence musicians and writers in later decades.

The Cold War became a theme of many popular novels in the 1950s. Spying and espionage were often in the news, and *Casino Royale*, Ian Fleming's first novel featuring James Bond, was published in 1953. Russian author Boris Pasternak's *Doctor Zhivago* was a success around the world but could only be distributed illegally in the author's home country at the time.[2]

Young people also had an impact on the best-seller lists. In the United States, these included books about youth and popular culture such as Jack Kerouac's *On the Road*. In the United Kingdom, many books by younger authors challenged Britain's old-fashioned class system.

George Orwell (1903-1950)

Eric Blair was born in India but moved to the United Kingdom as a child. He was educated at Eton, an exclusive private school, but his writing as George Orwell was often about the experience of working people and reflected his socialist views. Orwell made his name in the 1930s with books such as *The Road to Wigan Pier* (1937), which detailed the experience of working people during the Great Depression. His most popular and influential books were *Animal Farm* (1945) and *Nineteen Eighty-Four* (1949), which captured the mood of the times and the fears of the Cold War.[3]

Advances in color printing and the growing importance of advertising led to growth in magazine publishing, particularly aimed at women, in the 1950s. These magazines had to reflect changes in society and appeal to young women who were more interested in fashion and lifestyle features.

Science fiction

Popular science fiction books had been published since the nineteenth century, but science fiction grew more popular in the 1950s. Magazines like *Astounding Science Fiction*, which had started in the 1930s, and *The Magazine of Fantasy and Science Fiction*, first published in 1949, were a focus for science fiction enthusiasts, whose numbers were growing in the unfamiliar atmosphere of the Cold War.

Many of the most celebrated science fiction books were written in the 1950s. Isaac Asimov was one of the best authors of the genre. The stories he wrote for *Astounding Science Fiction* were collected as *I, Robot* (1950) and the *Foundation Series* (first volume published in 1951). Asimov was a scientist who also wrote nonfiction books and published more than 500 titles in his lifetime. Ray Bradbury was another star of the genre. His most famous works include *The Martian Chronicles* (1950) and *Fahrenheit 451* (1953), which is set in an imagined state where reading is forbidden and books are burned.[4] Popular British science fiction often had a more local focus, such as John Wyndham's *The Day of the Triffids* (1951), in which the United Kingdom is terrorized by giant, lethal plants.

Films and TV shows

In addition to the explosion in science fiction writing, there was also a boom in the number of science fiction films and TV programs. Most of these films were low-budget productions with unrealistic aliens and special effects. They were often designed to appeal to teenagers in the drive-in theaters. While many people took science fiction literature seriously, the production values of films and the quality of the sets only improved in later decades, when some of the most popular films and TV shows were adapted directly from science fiction writing.

Did you know?

The alternative world of J. R. R. Tolkien's *The Lord of the Rings*, first published between 1954 and 1955, shared some aspects with science fiction. The trilogy was mainly written during World War II, which influenced its tale of good versus evil. Although a moderate success when first published, its sales continued to increase in later years, and the books became some of the best-selling novels in history.[5]

Cold War inspiration

Science fiction writing is based on imagining an alternative world or future. This alternative reality could be created by technological or scientific change. The world of the Cold War provided plenty of inspiration for science fiction stories. There were new and horrifying nuclear weapons, the beginnings of space exploration when the Soviet Union launched the first unmanned satellite in 1957, and other technological marvels that were unthinkable even a few years before World War II. Fear of communism also had an influence on many stories of alien invasions and hidden enemies, as in the book and film *Invasion of the Body Snatchers* (published 1954, filmed 1955).[6]

Invasion of the Body Snatchers tells the story of a small California town where aliens take over the residents' bodies as they sleep.

Comics

Cartoon strips had long been featured in newspapers and continued to be popular. In 1947, the cartoon strip *Lil' Folks* was launched by Charles Schulz. In 1950, he changed the name of the strip to *Peanuts*. The first dedicated comic books that told a single story rather than collecting comic strips were published in the 1930s. Companies like DC and Marvel Comics established themselves as leaders in the genre.

During the war, comic books were popular as entertainment for troops overseas. Comics featuring superheroes such as Batman and Superman were sent from North America to Europe and were hugely popular, particularly because the British comics industry was affected by the war and paper rationing. Wonder Woman, the first female superhero, first appeared in 1941.[7] In addition to being humorous, comics also covered subjects such as crime and war stories.

A poll found that two-thirds of British adults favored a ban on importing violent American comics.

New comic genres

At the end of the 1940s, interest in superhero comics started to decline. Publishers like Marvel looked for the next new genre and started publishing western and romance comics. The two were even combined in titles like *Cowboy Romances*. These genres were only briefly popular. Publishers started producing comics in the areas of crime and horror. These were more popular but also fed growing concerns about whether the violence in these comics was affecting the readers. Following the introduction of the Comics Code (see box below), some comics publishers returned to the superhero genre that had proved itself in earlier decades. New heroes such as Spiderman started appearing in the early 1960s.

British and European comics

After the war, imports of U.S. comics into Britain were restricted, although publishers could reprint titles, including many of the horror titles that had been so controversial. Major British comics for children, including *The Beano* and *The Dandy*, resumed full publication only in 1949,[8] after the end of wartime paper rationing. They were joined by *The Eagle*, which was aimed at older readers. The comic featured interplanetary crime fighter Dan Dare, and was started by Christian groups as a response to what they saw as the dangers of crime and horror comics.[9]

Different styles of comics were also being developed across Europe. The character Tintin by the Belgian cartoonist Hergé had existed before World War II, but this comic came to new prominence with the launch of its own magazine in 1948.[10] The stories of the intrepid boy reporter later spread around the world. One of France's most famous characters, Asterix, was launched in 1959. Created by René Goscinny and Albert Uderzo, it has remained popular ever since.[11]

The Comics Code

Comics publishers found themselves under attack in the 1950s when psychologist Fredric Wertham claimed that violent comic books were corrupting America's youth and encouraging young men to turn to crime. Schools and parents were outraged and there were even examples of comics being publicly burned in protest. Eventually comics publishers agreed to follow strict rules, called the Comics Code, that severely restricted what they could include in comics. This had such an effect on the industry that many publishers closed down.[12]

The Birth of the Teenager?

In the 1950s, there was a new generation of teenagers who were too young to remember World War II. The word *teenager* was not new, but the 1950s were the first time that people really thought of the teenage years as a separate stage of life between childhood and adulthood. Although *teenager* literally refers to the years between the ages of 13 and 20, it can be taken to mean the period when young people are able to act independently and develop their own ideas, but do not yet have the responsibility of running their own home or family. During the 1950s, most young men in the United States and European countries had to serve a period of military service at the end of their teenage years.

Many young people were now spending more time in school and starting work later than previous generations had. When they finished education, jobs were available, which meant that they had more money than those who had grown up in previous decades.

Popular culture was a very important part of the lives of these teenagers. They could define their place in the world by the music they listened to, their favorite films, and the clothes they wore. In the mid-1950s, there were a number of films, such as *The Wild One* (1954), *Rebel Without a Cause* (1955), and *Blackboard Jungle* (1955), that were designed to appeal to young people, with images of teenage rebellion.

Blue jeans

Teenagers wore jeans as a reaction against the more formal clothes worn by their parents' generation. Denim jeans were first made in the 1800s by Levi Strauss and Co. They were designed to be tough working clothes, and rivets were added to make the pockets stronger. Jeans, which were then called waist overalls, were often used in western films. American soldiers took them overseas during World War II, and companies such as Wrangler and Lee started to make their own versions. In the 1950s, these working clothes became hugely popular with teenagers, who called them jean pants or jeans.[3]

Rock around the clock

Blackboard Jungle in particular caused a sensation when it arrived in Britain. The soundtrack included the song "Rock Around the Clock" by Bill Haley and the Comets. It soared to number one on the charts on November 24, 1955, and went on to become the first million-selling record in the United Kingdom.[1] The film and Haley's music led to riots of unruly teenagers in movie theaters, although the music itself was very tame compared with what was to come later from musicians such as Little Richard and Jerry Lee Lewis.

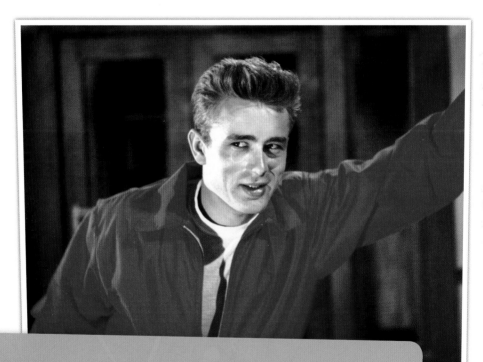

James Dean (1931–1955)

James Dean's reputation as an icon of teenage rebellion is a result of his starring roles in just three films. Dean was born in Marion, Indiana. After attending college in California he studied acting at the Actor's Studio, famous as the home of the method acting technique, in which actors immerse themselves in their roles. After appearing on Broadway, Dean was given his first starring role in *East of Eden* (1955). In the same year he filmed *Rebel Without a Cause*, his most famous performance as a brooding, troubled teenager. Dean's final film, *Giant*, was released in 1956, after his death in a car crash.[2]

The generation gap

Films that were popular with teenagers often included conflict between different generations. In *Rebel Without a Cause*, James Dean's character finds it difficult to communicate with his domineering mother and weak father. This was the first time that a generation gap had been clearly visible, from the clothes teenagers wore to the music they enjoyed.

In the affluent 1950s, there were more places where teenagers could meet their friends. Fast-food restaurants and diners appeared in the new suburbs where families were living. Outside the United States places to meet were more limited, although coffee bars aimed at young people were springing up in major cities. As well as eating, drinking, and meeting friends, teenagers might also listen to live music or the latest records on the jukebox. Jukeboxes would play a selected record for a small fee and were an important way for record companies to get their latest songs heard. Although there were radio stations playing rhythm and blues or rock and roll, most mainstream radio was still aimed at adult tastes.

The teenage market

Businesses and advertisers were quick to recognize that teenagers were potential customers for their goods. The success of rock and roll showed that teenagers had money for records and other forms of popular culture. TV programs aimed at teenagers, such as the dance show *American Bandstand*, could get huge audiences for advertisers. As businesses realized that there was money to be made, they set out to bring teenage culture into the mainstream.

Teens at a late-night diner in 1954. A jukebox is visible behind them. Jukeboxes provided young people with access to new music and entertainment during the 1950s.

As the first frenzy of rock and roll faded, Elvis Presley went to Hollywood to make films that the whole family could watch. New stars were promoted who owed almost as much to the crooners of a previous generation as they did to the excitement of rhythm and blues. It seemed as if rock and roll and teenage rebellion might just be a passing fad. However, the teenager would not prove so easy to control as the next generation took up the baton from the 1950s.

Teddy boys and girls

Teddy boy style began in Britain during the 1950s. These teenagers, usually of the working class, wore distinctive clothes and hairstyles that were intended to copy styles worn by the upper classes. Teddy was short for "Edwardians," which these teens were originally called because their clothes were thought to mimic styles from the Edwardian period (the early 1900s). They were also influenced by images of the American West, which reached the United Kingdom through films and television. With their long jackets, narrow trousers, and hair worn long on top and at the back, teddy boys were very distinctive and were often seen as threatening by older generations.

Quote

"What're you rebelling against, Johnny?"

"Whaddya got?"

Marlon Brando's reply in *The Wild One* expresses the teenage rebellion of the 1950s

Changing Times

It would have been very difficult for people living though the darkest days of World War II in 1940 to imagine the relative wealth that the average family would enjoy in the late 1950s. It would also have been difficult to imagine, as they listened to news of the war on the radio, the impact that television would have on society and popular culture. However, the major changes of this period did not happen all at once.

Change in the 1940s

The war years were in many ways a continuation of the Great Depression of the 1930s. Although war brought people jobs that had not been there in the previous decade, many goods were in short supply, particularly in Britain and Europe. Resources were directed to the war effort rather than to innovation in popular culture, and people relied on the dance bands and books that they had enjoyed in the 1930s.

In the late 1940s, television and long-playing records became available, but it would be a few years before they had an impact. The war cast a long shadow, not just because of the horrors of the Holocaust and the atomic bomb, but also because of the cost of reconstruction in Europe and Asia. The start of the Cold War also gave rise to fear of communism and the first witch hunts for communist sympathizers in Hollywood.

The spread of modern conveniences like the refrigerator meant that people had more time for leisure.

The 1950s boom

In the 1950s, changes in technology and booming economies led to big changes in many areas of popular culture. Television started to become part of every living room, forcing the film industry to adapt. Science fiction authors and films explored where technology would take society. Teenagers began to develop their own distinctive pop culture.

American dominance

During this period, many American troops remained in Europe well after the end of the war and brought exciting new products with them. Much of the music of the period, from swing to rhythm and blues, came from the United States, although local musicians would adopt and adapt the styles for their own audiences. Pop culture in many countries was dominated by American films, music, and other products more than ever before.

Fads and crazes

Technology played a large part in changing popular culture in the 1950s. Not every invention can change the world, but technology had a hand in developing many different products.

- Hula hoops: The light and flexible hoop made from new plastic was first sold by Alex Tolmer in Australia. After the hoop was introduced in the United States in 1958, 100 million were sold in just two years.[1]
- Frisbee: Fred Morrison developed a light, aerodynamic flying disk, which he called the Flyin-Saucer and then the Pluto Platter. The Wham-O company bought the rights and changed its name to the Frisbee in 1957.[2]
- Polaroid camera: the first instant camera, developed by Edwin Land using ideas he had developed while working for the military during World War II.[3]

51

What Did the 1940s and 1950s Do for Us?

In many ways the 1940s and 1950s were a different world. Global war and Cold War tension meant that this was a very uncertain time. Although more women worked during the war, roles for men and women in the family were still quite traditional. African Americans in the southern United States still did not enjoy the same rights as white citizens, and racial prejudice was common far beyond this region.

Multimedia has come a long way since the 1940s and 1950s. Personal computers and mobile phones were the stuff of science fiction, and the first televisions were a long way from the high-definition flat screens we are used to now. However, in many different ways the pop culture of the postwar period paved the way for the culture we enjoy today.

Little Richard (shown at the piano) was one of the great showmen of rock and roll whose influence is still felt today.

Roots of modern music

Rhythm and blues remains the foundation for most of the popular music we listen to today, whether through the rock and roll that led to white rock music or the mostly black music that developed, such as soul, funk, and hip-hop. The jazz, country, and folk music of the 1940s and 1950s have also been a major influence on modern artists.

Blockbusters

The film industry also began to take the shape that we recognize today, with Hollywood focusing on producing a limited number of blockbuster movies that they could sell to movie theaters to tempt people away from their TVs. These blockbusters were often films of popular books. Today's blockbusters, such as the *Harry Potter* films or movies based on comic book superheroes, are often built on characters that have been established in print.

Home and family

The homes of the 1950s, with their emphasis on colorful design, modern gadgets, and new materials such as plastics, would be much more familiar to us today than those of 20 years earlier. Home entertainment would also be familiar, with television, small transistor radios, and recorded music, although CDs and MP3s have largely replaced the records of the 1950s.

We would also recognize the lives of 1950s teenagers much more than we would the teens of the previous generation. It is now common for different generations to have different clothes and tastes in pop culture.

Disneyland

In 1955, Walt Disney opened his first theme park in Anaheim, California. Disneyland included different themed areas based around periods from U.S. history or Disney films. Many people questioned whether the park, which charged $1 for an adult ticket, would be a success.[5] Since then, theme parks have become an important part of modern pop culture.

Timeline

Year	Popular culture	World events
1940	Charlie Chaplin's *The Great Dictator* (film)	Winston Churchill becomes British Prime Minister Netherlands, Belgium, and France invaded by Germany Battle of Britain
1941	*Citizen Kane* (film) Vera Lynn, "We'll Meet Again" (music)	(December 7) Japan attacks U.S. fleet at Pearl Harbor, Hawaii United States and Soviet Union enter World War II
1942	*Casablanca, Bambi* (films) Frank Sinatra becomes solo performer	
1943	Rodgers and Hammerstein's *Oklahoma!* staged on Broadway	Allied forces begin invasion of Italy
1944	Laurence Olivier's *Henry V* (film) Bandleader Glenn Miller's plane disappears while traveling to France	(June 6) D-Day: Allied forces begin invasion of Europe
1945	George Orwell, *Animal Farm* (novel) First regular TV service in United States Marriage of Humphrey Bogart and Lauren Bacall	(May 8) VE Day: end of World War II in Europe (August 15) Japan surrenders after explosion of atomic bombs at Hiroshima and Nagasaki Harry S. Truman becomes U.S. president
1946	Louis Jordan, "Choo Choo Ch'Boogie" (music) Record year for movie attendance	
1947	Christian Dior launches the New Look Hollywood Ten jailed for refusing to cooperate with HUAC investigation	Indian independence and establishment of Pakistan Invention of transistor radio
1948	Long-playing record and 45 rpm single launched	State of Israel declared. Arab-Israeli conflict begins.
1949	George Orwell, *Nineteen Eighty-Four* (novel) *South Pacific* (musical) Billboard magazine includes rhythm and blues charts for the first time	Communist People's Republic of China declared

1950	*Watch With Mother* begins on UK TV	Korean War begins
	Isaac Asimov, *I, Robot* (novel)	
1951	J. D. Salinger, *The Catcher in the Rye* (novel)	
	I Love Lucy begins on U.S. TV	
1952	*Singin' in the Rain* (film)	Accession of Queen Elizabeth II
	Alan Freed uses the phrase "rock 'n' roll" in the title of his radio show	
1953	Ray Bradbury, *Fahrenheit 451* (novel)	Dwight D. Eisenhower becomes U.S. president
	Death of country star Hank Williams	Korean War ends
	Ray Charles, "Mess Around" (music)	
1954	Commercial television launched in United Kingdom	Racial segregation in U.S. schools declared unconstitutional
	On the Waterfront (film)	
1955	*Rebel Without a Cause* (film)	Rosa Parks sits in a "whites only" seat on an Alabama bus, sparking the Montgomery Bus Boycott
	Elvis Presley signs for RCA records	
	Little Richard, "Tutti Frutti" (music)	
1956	Elvis Presley, "Heartbreak Hotel" (music)	Suez Crisis when United Kingdom and France attempt to gain control of Suez Canal
	Frank Sinatra, "Songs for Swingin' Lovers" (music)	
	Grace Kelly marries Prince Rainier of Monaco	
1957	*West Side Story* (stage musical)	First unmanned satellite launched by Soviet Union
	Jack Kerouac, *On the Road* (novel)	
1958	Cliff Richard, "Move It" (music)	
	Hula hoop introduced in the United States	
1959	*Some Like It Hot* (film)	U.S. satellite takes first TV pictures of Earth
	Buddy Holly, Ritchie Valens, and the Big Bopper killed in plane crash	
	Goscinny and Uderzo's Asterix launched	

Best of the Era

The best way to find out about the pop culture of the 1940s and 1950s is to experience it for yourself. Here are some suggestions for the best or most typical examples that will give you a sense of the time.

Movies

Bambi (1942): Hugely successful animated film produced by Walt Disney.

Citizen Kane (1941): Orson Welles's story of a newspaper tycoon.

Casablanca (1942): Classic romance set in wartime Morocco.

Singin' in the Rain (1952): Hit musicals were a feature of cinema in the 1950s, and Gene Kelly's story of an earlier era in Hollywood is one of the best.

From Here to Eternity (1953): Wartime romance.

On the Waterfront (1954): Elia Kazan's tale of New York dockworkers.

Rear Window (1954): Thriller about a murderer too close to home.

Seven Samurai (1954): Akira Kurosawa's classic Japanese film was remade in Hollywood as the western *The Magnificent Seven* (1960).

Rebel Without a Cause (1955): The ultimate film of teenage rebellion.

The Ladykillers (1955): A great example of Ealing comedy, made at Ealing Studios in London. A gang of criminals led by Alec Guinness plan a bank robbery while living with the aging Mrs. Wilberforce.

The Searchers (1956): Western starring John Wayne.

Some Like It Hot (1959): Jack Lemmon and Tony Curtis as "Daphne" and "Josephine" join an all-girl band on tour in Florida, which also features Marilyn Monroe. What could possibly go wrong?

Ben Hur (1959): Blockbuster tale of chariot racing in ancient Rome.

Music

Duke Ellington: Genius of jazz music with a five-decade career.

Frank Sinatra: The first pop star?

Hank Williams: The biggest star in the history of country music.

Ray Charles: Ray Charles's career included many different styles, but his recordings for Atlantic Records in the 1950s made his name.

Ella Fitzgerald: One of the greatest singers of all time.

Elvis Presley: Hugely popular early rock and roll star.

Chuck Berry: Berry wrote some of the greatest rock-and-roll songs, and was probably the first guitar hero.

Little Richard: Known for purely exciting and riotous performances.

Cliff Richard (no relation to Little Richard!): Cliff's polite brand of rock and roll was the closest that British audiences could get to the big U.S. stars. He soon left rock and roll behind for a career as a family entertainer.

Television

Dragnet: Hugely popular police series.

The Ed Sullivan Show: TV variety show that was known for iconic performances such as the appearance of Elvis Presley (1956).

Gunsmoke: Western drama series.

Hancock's Half Hour: The British version of situation comedy.

I Love Lucy: The show that pioneered TV situation comedy.

Books

Isaac Asimov, *I, Robot* (1950): One example of the huge range of science fiction published in the 1940s and 1950s.

Ian Fleming, *Casino Royale* (1953): The first novel about Cold War secret agent James Bond.

George Orwell, *Nineteen Eighty-Four* (1949): Orwell's tale of Cold War paranoia is just as relevant today.

Jack Kerouac, *On the Road* (1957): Semi-autobiographical novel that has come to represent the beat generation.

J. D. Salinger, *The Catcher in the Rye* (1951): Classic novel of youthful rebellion.

John Wyndham, *The Day of the Triffids* (1951): British version of science fiction.

Miscellaneous

Comics: Look for the superhero comics from the period and other examples such as Hergé's *The Adventures of Tintin*.

Design: There are lots of examples of classic 1950s design from jukeboxes to classic American cars.

The Goon Show: Bizarre radio comedy that influenced many later comedians.

Rodgers and Hammerstein: Movies were made of many of these musicals and they are often revived on Broadway and in the West End of London.

Wartime propaganda posters: These often used the finest designers and artists of the time to create clear and stylish messages for a mass audience.

Notes on Sources

What Is Popular Culture?

1. Peter Guralnick, *Last Train to Memphis: The Rise of Elvis Presley* (London: Abacus, 1995), 337–38.

2. *Time* magazine, "Who Built the First Computer?", March 29, 1999, http://www.time.com/time/magazine/article/0,9171,990596,00.html

Culture in the Shadow of War

1. I.C.B. Dear and M.R.D. Foot, eds., "BBC," *The Oxford Companion to World War II* (Oxford: Oxford University Press, 2001); Oxford Reference Online, http://www.oxfordreference.com/views/ENTRY.html?subview=Main&entry=t129.e147.

2. BBC News, "1954: Housewives Celebrate End of Rationing," http://news.bbc.co.uk/onthisday/hi/dates/stories/july/4/newsid_3818000/3818563.stm.

3. Donald Clarke, ed., *Penguin Encyclopedia of Popular Music* (London: Penguin Books, 1990), 731; Encyclopaedia Britannica, s.v. "Vera Lynn," http://library.eb.co.uk/eb/article-9544540?query=lynn%2C%20vera&ct=.

4. Hugh Brogan, *Pelican History of the United States of America* (London: Pelican, 1986), 648.

Going to the Movies

1. Ronald Bergan, *Eyewitness Companion: Film* (London: Dorling Kindersley, 2006), 37.

2. David Kynaston, *A World to Build: Austerity Britain 1945–48* (London: Bloomsbury, 2007), 95.

3. Harold Evans, *The American Century* (London: Jonathan Cape, 1998), 440.

4. Bergan, *Eyewitness Companion*, 37.

5. Bergan, *Eyewitness Companion*, 306–307; *History of the Twentieth Century, Vol. 6: The Cold War Years* (London: Hamlyn, 2003), 161.

6. A.M. Sperber and Eric Lax, "Bogart and Bacall," *Vanity Fair*, February 1997, http://www.vanityfair.com/hollywood/features/1997/02/bogart-bacall-excerpt-199702?currentPage=1.

7. BBC News, "1956: Prince Rainier Marries Grace Kelly," http://news.bbc.co.uk/onthisday/hi/dates/stories/april/19/newsid_2720000/2720723.stm.

8. *History of the Twentieth Century, Vol. 6: The Cold War Years*, 149.

Home Entertainment

1. Anthony Smith, ed., *Television: An International History* (Oxford: Oxford University Press, 1995), 31.

2. Kynaston, *A World to Build: Austerity Britain 1945-48*, 212.

3. Encyclopaedia Britannica, s.v. "Broadcasting," http://library.eb.co.uk/eb/article-25190.

4. Kynaston, *A World to Build*, 212.

5. Encyclopaedia Britannica, s.v. "Transistor," http://library.eb.co.uk/eb/article-236464.

6. Quote from Lennon's review of The Goon Show Scripts for *New York Times*, 1972, http://www.thegoonshow.net/tributes/john_lennon.asp.

7. Smith, *Television*, 38.

8. Smith, *Television*, 40.

9. Smith, *Television*, 84.

10. Smith, *Television*, 84.

11. Encyclopaedia Britannica, s.v. "Television," http://library.eb.co.uk/eb/article-25147.

12. Bergan, *Eyewitness Companion: Film*, 45.

13. *Time*, "The Time 100: Lucille Ball," June 8, 1998, http://www.time.com/time/time100/artists/profile/lucy.html.

14. Encyclopaedia Britannica, s.v. "Lucille Ball," http://library.eb.co.uk/eb/article-9011982?query=lucille%20ball&ct=null.

Music

1. Clarke, *Penguin Encyclopedia of Popular Music*, 107.

2. Clarke, *Penguin Encyclopedia of Popular Music*, 1073-76, and Encyclopaedia Britannica, s.v. "Frank Sinatra," http://library.eb.co.uk/eb/article-9067897.

3. Clarke, *Penguin Encyclopedia of Popular Music*, 1074.

4. Julia Sutton, et al. "Dance," Grove Music Online; Oxford Music Online, http://www.oxfordmusiconline.com/subscriber/article/grove/music/45795.

5. John Snelson and Andrew Lamb, "Musical," Grove Music Online; Oxford Music Online, http://www.oxfordmusiconline.com/subscriber/article/grove/music/19420.

6. Snelson and Lamb, "Musical"; Oxford Music Online, http://www.oxfordmusiconline.com/subscriber/article/grove/music/19420.

7. Clarke, *Penguin Encyclopedia of Popular Music*, 1000-01.

8. Clarke, *Penguin Encyclopedia of Popular Music*, 289.

9. Clarke, *Penguin Encyclopedia of Popular Music*, 1078.

10. Clarke, *Penguin Encyclopedia of Popular Music*, 227.

11. *History of the Twentieth Century, Vol. 6: The Cold War Years*, 140.

12. Clarke, *Penguin Encyclopedia of Popular Music*, 225-26.

13. George, Nelson, *The Death of Rhythm and Blues* (London: Omnibus Press, 1989), 70-71.

14. Guralnick, *Last Train to Memphis*, 338.

Design and Clothes

1. BBC History Online, "Make Do and Mend," http://www.bbc.co.uk/history/trail/wars_conflict/home_front/the_home_front_10.shtml.

2. Jonathan Woodham, s.v. "Nylon," *A Dictionary of Modern Design* (Oxford: Oxford University Press, 2004); Oxford Reference Online, http://www.oxfordreference.com/views/ENTRY.html?subview=Main&entry=t160.e599.

3. Encyclopaedia Britannica, s.v. "Bayerische Motoren Werke AG (BMW)," http://library.eb.co.uk/eb/article-9013870.

4. *History of the Twentieth Century, Vol. 6: The Cold War Years*, 133.

5. CBS.com, http://www.cbs.com/daytime/as_the_world_turns/about/?sec=4.

The Printed Word

1. Encyclopaedia Britannica, s.v. "Publishing, history of," http://library.eb.co.uk/eb/article-28645.

2. John Sutherland, *Bestsellers: A Very Short Introduction* (Oxford: Oxford University Press, 2007), 67.

3. Margaret Drabble, ed., *Oxford Companion to English Literature* (Oxford: Oxford University Press, 1995), 732–33.

4. Dinah Birch, ed., s.v. "Bradbury, Ray," *Oxford Companion to English Literature*, (Oxford: Oxford University Press); Oxford Reference Online, http://www.oxfordreference.com/views/ENTRY.html?subview=Main&entry=t113.e998, Accessed June 3, 2011.

5. David Doughan, J.R.R. Tolkien: A Biographical Sketch, The Tolkien Society Web Site, http://www.tolkiensociety.org/tolkien/biography.html.

6. Encyclopaedia Britannica, s.v. "Science fiction," http://library.eb.co.uk/eb/article-235723.

7. Encyclopaedia Britannica, s.v. "Wonder Woman," http://library.eb.co.uk/eb/article-9443955?query=wonder%20woman&ct=null.

8. Tim Pilcher and Brad Brooks, *Essential Guide to World Comics* (London: Collins and Brown, 2005), 63.

9. Pilcher and Brooks, *Essential Guide to World Comics*, 63–5.

10. Pilcher and Brooks, *Essential Guide to World Comics*, 150.

11. Pilcher and Brooks, *Essential Guide to World Comics*, 153.

12. Pilcher and Brooks, *Essential Guide to World Comics*, 28.

The Birth of the Teenager?

1. Kynaston, *Family Britain 1951–57*, 605.

2. *Who's Who in the Twentieth Century* (Oxford: Oxford University Press, 1999), s.v. "Dean, James"; Oxford Reference Online, http://www.oxfordreference.com/views/ENTRY.html?subview=Main&entry=t47.e451.

3. University of Rhode Island, "The History of Jeans," http://www.uri.edu/personal/svon6141/history.htm.

Changing Times

1. Enyclopaedia Britannica, s.v. "Hula hoop," http://library.eb.co.uk/eb/article-9475178?query=hula%20hoop&ct=.

2. *Los Angeles Times*, "Walter Fredrick Morrison Dies at 90; Father of the Frisbee," February 13, 2010, http://www.latimes.com/news/obituaries/la-me-fred-morrison13-2010feb13,0,7076853.story.

3. Encyclopaedia Britannica, s.v. "Edwin Herbert Land," http://library.eb.co.uk/eb/article-9047025.

4. Kynaston, *A World to Build: Austerity Britain 1945-48*, 94.

5. *Los Angeles Times*, "Disneyland: From orange groves to Magic Kingdom," May 18, 2005, http://articles.latimes.com/2005/may/18/local/me-disneyland18.

Find Out More

Books

Bergan, Ronald. *Film* (Eyewitness Companion). New York: Dorling Kindersley, 2006.

Cregan, Elizabeth R. *Independence and Equality* (World Black History). Chicago: Raintree, 2009.

Guillain, Charlotte. *Music* (Timeline History). Chicago: Raintree, 2010.

Harrison, Paul. *The 1950s* (Dates of a Decade). New York: Franklin Watts, 2008.

Walker, Kathryn. *My Family Remembers the 1950s*. New York: Franklin Watts, 2011.

Websites

kclibrary.lonestar.edu/decades.html
This site gives details and images about American pop culture in each decade of the twentieth century.

www.badfads.com/home.html
The "Bad Fads Museum" is a lighthearted site that brings together some of the most interesting and unlikely fads and crazes from the history of popular culture, including drive-in movies and Frisbees.

rockhall.com
The Rock and Roll Hall of Fame includes information, music, and video about some of the pioneers of rock and roll.

www.npg.si.edu/exhibit/elvis
The Smithsonian Institution is a great resource for information on all sorts of pop culture topics. Follow this link to find an exhibition about Elvis Presley or go to http://www.si.edu for the home page of the Smithsonian.

www.life.com/archive/timeline/decade/1950
Media from the period can give a real sense of what life was like. *Life* magazine's website includes many photographic timelines from this and other periods.

Other resources

People in the 1940s and 1950s could go to the movies and watch TV, but they did not have the opportunity to watch DVDs or online videos of their pop culture. Films and TV programs like many of those mentioned in this book can tell you a huge amount about the period.

One of the best ways to find out about recent history is to talk to the people who lived through it. Your grandparents or other older relatives may remember what life was like for them in the 1940s and 1950s and can tell you about what they experienced.

Topics for further research

- The home front: Finding examples of popular culture during wartime can give great insight into the conditions that people faced during World War II.
- Civil rights: The rise of rhythm and blues happened against the background of the battle for civil rights in the United States. Find out more about pop culture and politics in this period.
- Look at other cultural movements of the period. What was happening in art, theater, classical music, and literature? Did these influence pop culture or were they affected by what was happening in the mass media?

Glossary

affluent relatively wealthy

austerity spending as little money as possible

blockbuster film or book that is hugely successful

box office part of a cinema or theater where you buy tickets, also used to describe the total money that customers pay to see a film or other event

brand product made by a particular maker or company, often with a distinctive mark to show who it is made by. Companies try to persuade people to think that their brands are better than other products.

Broadway street in New York City that is the home of theater and musical shows, also used as an adjective to describe major theater productions

capitalist capitalism is an economic system that depends on people investing capital (money) to make and sell products. The people who invest money are capitalists.

censorship restricting what people are allowed to see or read

civil rights rights that citizens have in a country, such as in a democracy most people have the right to vote in elections

Cold War period of tension and military threats between the United States and the Soviet Union, each supported by their allies. The Cold War lasted from the end of World War II to about 1991.

commercial anything that is designed to make money, also used to mean TV advertising

communist someone who believes that all property should be controlled by the government, with everyone working for the state. There were communist governments in much of Eastern Europe, the Soviet Union, and China during the second half of the twentieth century.

consumer anyone who buys or uses the products made by businesses, including products like music and films

consumerism idea that consuming things, such as buying the latest goods, is an important part of society

cover version copy of a song produced by an artist other than the person or group who originally wrote or recorded the song

cult something that attracts a small group of very enthusiastic followers

democratic a form of government which is voted for by the people of a country or region

director person who directs or controls the making of a film or television program

equality being equal, particularly when applied to different genders or races of people

escapism distraction from unpleasant realties

Great Depression period of great economic hardship and unemployment that happened in many parts of the world, including the United States and Europe, in the 1930s

Holocaust systematic persecution and murder of millions of Jewish people by Nazi Germany during World War II

medium (singular) means of communication. The plural term "media" describes all the means of mass communication, such as TV and newspapers.

morale mental outlook of a person or group. For example in wartime, people often have low morale.

network group of television or radio stations that broadcast the same programs in their local area, such as the CBS, NBC, and ABC networks in U.S. television

Oscar statuette given to winners of categories at the U.S. Academy Awards. Oscars are awarded in many categories, including films, directors, and actors.

persecution mistreatment of others and targeting others for mistreatment

propaganda information that is designed to present a particular point of view, such as that held by the government, and excludes or ignores information that disagrees with that view

racist someone who discriminates against people because of where they come from, their background, or the color of their skin

ration restrict availability of something, such as food or clothes, often because of limited supplies

role model someone who sets an example for others of how to behave

segregation state or action in which people are set apart in different groups

suburb residential district away from the center of a city

transistor tiny switch used in many electronic devices, including radios and computers

tycoon powerful and wealthy businessperson

variety show form of entertainment mixing comedy, music, and dance

versatile adaptable, with many uses

witch hunt campaign of persecution against a group, particularly because of the views they hold

Index